INNSBRUCK CHRISTMAS

Vacation Guide 2023

" Innsbruck Festive Charm, A Christmas and New year showcase in Austria"

Earl C Wilson

Copyright © 2023 by Earl C. Wilson

All rights reserved.

No part of this publication may be reproduced, distributed, or transmitted in any form or by any means, including photocopying, recording, or other electronic or mechanical methods, without the prior written permission of the publisher, except in the case of brief quotations embodied in critical reviews and certain other noncommercial uses permitted

Table of Contents

1. INTRODUCTION.. 3

2. PLANNING YOUR TRIP......................................8

3. EXPLORING INNSBRUCK............................. 14

4. CHRISTMAS TRADITIONS..............................20

5. CHRISTMAS MARKETS.................................. 25

6. CULINARY DELIGHTS..................................... 31

7. INNSBRUCK NIGHTLIFE............................... 36

8. CHRISTMAS EVE AND NEW YEAR'S EVE CELEBRATIONS.. 41

9. DAY TRIPS & EXCURSIONS........................... 49

10. PRACTICAL INFORMATION........................ 53

11. CONCLUSION.. 59

1. INTRODUCTION

Welcome to Innsbruck Christmas Magic

Welcome to a city that symbolizes the festive spirit like no other — Innsbruck, where Christmas comes alive with an exquisite blend of tradition, natural beauty, and cultural depth. Nestled in the heart of the Tyrolean Alps, Innsbruck is a canvas of snow-covered mountains, medieval architecture, and lively marketplaces. The city changes into a winter paradise throughout the Christmas season, enticing visitors with its festive beauty.

As you arrive in Innsbruck, you'll be met by the wonderful aroma of roasted chestnuts and the cheerful sounds of carolers. Every corner is decked with shimmering lights, giving a pleasant glow on the cobbled streets. Whether you're drawn to the centuries-old traditions or the spectacular winter sports, Innsbruck has something to offer every traveler seeking a wonderful Christmas experience.

1.2 Overview of Innsbruck

Innsbruck, the capital of Tyrol in western Austria, is a city rich in history and surrounded by spectacular natural beauty. Situated in a valley along the Inn River, Innsbruck has long been a crossroads of cultures, making it a unique blend of Austrian history and international influence.

The city's architecture is a monument to its historic past, with Gothic and Baroque buildings standing alongside modern skyscrapers. Innsbruck's historical Old Town, known as the Altstadt, is a labyrinth of small alleyways and colorful facades, affording a look into its medieval background.

1.3 History and Culture

Innsbruck's history extends back over a thousand years, with roots as a bridgehead and trading town. It earned renown as the palace of the Habsburgs, one of Europe's most powerful royal families. This rich history is intertwined into the fabric of the city, from the Imperial Palace to the Golden Roof, a symbol of Innsbruck's golden age during the Renaissance.

Cultural diversity is a characteristic of Innsbruck. The city's proximity to Italy and Germany has impacted its identity, expressed in its language, cuisine, and customs. This confluence of cultures is highlighted during the holiday season, where tourists may enjoy a tapestry of traditions from across the region.

1.4 Geography and Climate

Nestled in the heart of the Austrian Alps, Innsbruck is surrounded by breathtaking peaks that create a stunning backdrop to the city. The Nordkette mountain range, accessible by a funicular, affords stunning views of the city and the Inn Valley.

Innsbruck experiences a continental alpine climate, typified by cold winters and pleasant summers. During the Christmas season, the city is generally covered in a layer of snow, creating a lovely scene for holiday celebrations.

1.5 About This Guide

This guide is designed to be your trusted companion on your Innsbruck Christmas experience. It's intended to provide you with all the knowledge you need to make the most of your stay, ensuring that every minute is filled with wonder and excitement.

Each component of this guide is expertly crafted to give insights, ideas, and recommendations, covering everything from experiencing the city's lovely Christmas markets to immersing yourself in its rich cultural legacy. Whether you're a history buff, an outdoor enthusiast, or a lover of traditional festivals, there's something here for everyone.

1.6 A Glimpse of 2023 Christmas Showcase and New Year in Australia

While Innsbruck is a jewel of Christmas magic, it's worth remembering that Australia also possesses a unique manner of celebrating the holiday season. Down under, Christmas falls during the height of summer, delivering an altogether different experience. From celebratory beach barbecues to breathtaking fireworks displays, Australia promises a celebration that's as bright and diverse as its terrain.

In this guide, we'll offer a glimpse into the thrilling Christmas and New Year celebrations awaiting you in Australia. Whether you're drawn to the iconic fireworks over Sydney Harbour or the calm seaside festivities, you'll discover a multitude of options to ring in the new year in true Australian style. So, whether you're planning a multi-destination holiday or simply curious about what the southern hemisphere has to offer, stay tuned for a taste of the festive season 'down under'.

2. PLANNING YOUR TRIP

Getting Ready for Your Trip

Embarking on a wonderful journey to Innsbruck during the Christmas season demands meticulous preparation. From choosing the ideal time for your stay to packing basics, this area is committed to ensuring you have everything in place for a flawless and pleasurable holiday experience.

2.1 Best Time to Visit

Innsbruck comes alive during the Christmas season, which normally extends from late November through early January. The city is transformed into a magical winter wonderland, with festive decorations, bustling markets, and a palpable sense of holiday cheer. The season between late November and mid-December is particularly captivating, as it offers a mix between the holiday spirit and relatively fewer visitors. However, if you're an experienced skier or snowboarder, extending your stay into January allows you to take full advantage of the winter sports season.

2.2 Duration of Stay

The optimal duration of your stay in Innsbruck mostly relies on your interests and the experiences you intend to immerse yourself in. A minimum of three to four days is recommended to tour the city's Christmas markets, and cultural attractions, and indulge in winter sports. If you're an outdoor enthusiast intent on hitting the slopes, extending your stay to a week provides you with a more thorough ski or snowboarding vacation.

2.3 Accommodation Options

Innsbruck offers a varied choice of housing options to suit all interests and budgets. The city boasts a collection of beautiful boutique hotels, situated in old buildings with characterful décor. For those seeking a more private experience, holiday rentals and chalets in the nearby countryside provide a comfortable hideaway. Additionally, prominent international hotel brands are offering modern amenities and services. It's advisable to reserve accommodation well in advance, especially during the peak Christmas season, to ensure your favorite choice.

2.4 Communication and Internet Access

While German is the official language of Australia, English is frequently used in Innsbruck, particularly in tourist areas and among the younger population. You'll discover that most signs, menus, and information in public locations are available in both German and English. Additionally, many hotels and restaurants have English-speaking staff. In terms of internet connectivity, Innsbruck is well-connected, with most hotels, cafes, and public spaces offering free Wi-Fi. If you like to have constant internet access during your travel, try getting a local SIM card or portable Wi-Fi gadget.

2.5 Visa and Travel Requirements

For most passengers, a Schengen Visa is necessary to enter Austria, which enables access to all Schengen nations. Ensure that your passport is valid for at least six months beyond your scheduled travel date. Check with the Austrian consulate or embassy in your country for unique visa requirements and application procedures. Travel insurance is also highly advised to cover unforeseen circumstances such as travel cancellations, medical emergencies, and lost luggage.

2.6 How to Get to Innsbruck

Innsbruck is easily accessible by plane, train, and road. The Innsbruck Kranebitten Airport (INN) is the closest airport, located around 5 kilometers from the city center. It offers both domestic and international flights, with major European cities giving direct connections. From the airport, you can reach the city center via taxi, airport shuttle, or public transit. Alternatively, if you're traveling from nearby European countries, train services provide a scenic and convenient choice.

2.7 Local Transportation

Innsbruck features an efficient and reliable public transit system, including trams and buses, making it easy to travel to the city and its surroundings. The Innsbruck Card, available for purchase, gives unlimited travel on public transit and grants access to different attractions and incentives. If you plan to explore the wider Tyrol region or take day trips, consider hiring a car, which offers you more flexibility and access to distant regions.

2.8 Christmas Travel Packing Tips

Packing for a Christmas trip to Innsbruck involves careful consideration of the winter environment and festive activities. Essential things include warm clothes such as insulated jackets, thermal layers, gloves, and robust waterproof boots for outdoor adventure. Don't forget to carry a decent-quality camera to record the lovely moments. Additionally, prepare a formal dress if you plan to attend special holiday activities or performances. Lastly, remember to include a power adapter if your gadgets have multiple plug types, ensuring you stay connected throughout your travel.

By paying attention to five crucial parts of preparation, you'll create the foundation for a rewarding and joyful Christmas vacation in Innsbruck. From finding accommodation to packing adequately, each step ensures that you're well-equipped to make the most of this magical holiday season.

3. EXPLORING INNSBRUCK

Innsbruck, a city set in the heart of the Tyrolean Alps, provides a plethora of experiences for travelers eager to explore its rich history, vibrant culture, and magnificent natural surroundings. This section digs into the must-visit sights, cultural activities, outdoor excursions, and hidden jewels that await those who go into this charming Austrian city.

3.1 Must-visit Attractions

1. Imperial Palace (Hofburg): The Imperial Palace, or Hofburg, is a testimony to Innsbruck's historical prominence. Once the residence of the mighty Habsburgs, this enormous building contains lavish apartments, historical furnishings, and the famous Giant's Hall. The Imperial

Apartments provide a stunning peek into the luxurious lifestyle of the royal family.

2. Golden Roof (Goldenes Dachl): An iconic landmark of Innsbruck, the Golden Roof is a marvel of Gothic architecture. Adorned with thousands of gilded copper tiles, it previously functioned as the balcony from which Emperor Maximilian I watched contests in the square below. The Golden Roof Museum showcases the history and significance of this beautiful monument.

3. Ambras Castle (Schloss Ambras): Nestled in a lovely park, Ambras Castle is a treasure trove of art, history, and culture. Its collections include a large array of armor and weaponry, along with the Chamber of Art and Curiosities, a remarkable assortment of Renaissance antiques. The castle's grounds and magnificent vistas of Innsbruck are equally appealing.

3.2 Cultural Experiences

1. Tyrolean Folk Art Museum (Tiroler Volkskunstmuseum): This museum offers a thorough dive into the Tyrolean culture, presenting a broad variety of traditional antiques, including clothes, furniture, and religious art. Intricately crafted cribs and folk costumes provide a vivid portrait of the region's heritage.

2. Innsbruck State Theater (Tiroler Landestheater): For a taste of the local performing arts scene, a visit to the Innsbruck State Theater is a must. Hosting a range of shows from opera and ballet to drama and musicals, this cultural hub provides an opportunity to immerse yourself in the thriving arts community of Innsbruck.

3.3 Outdoor Adventures

1. Nordkette Mountain Range: Innsbruck's backyard lies the awe-inspiring Nordkette mountain range, easily accessible via the Nordkette Cable Car.

 Hike or enjoy a stroll along the well-marked trails for stunning panoramic views of the city and the Inn Valley. In winter, this area changes into a wonderland for snow sports aficionados.

2. Bergisel Ski Jump and Museum: A blend of modern architecture and sporting tradition, the Bergisel Ski Jump is an exciting attraction. Take an elevator to the summit for stunning views or visit the museum to learn about the sport of ski jumping and the legendary events performed here.

3.4 Hidden Gems

1. Wilten Basilica (Stift Wilten): Tucked away in the Wilten area, this Baroque beauty is sometimes overlooked by tourists. The church features a magnificent interior with elaborate murals, ornate altars, and a calm ambiance. The nearby monastery and grounds offer a calm refuge from the hectic city.

2. Hofgarten: This magnificent Renaissance garden, located behind the Imperial Palace, is a quiet sanctuary in the center of Innsbruck. Designed in the 16th century, it boasts manicured lawns, symmetrical flower beds, and a central pavilion. It's a perfect area for a stroll or a time of peaceful thought.

Exploring Innsbruck is an engaging adventure through history, culture, and environment. Whether you're attracted by the grandeur of imperial palaces, drawn to the arts, or keen to embark on outdoor activities, Innsbruck provides an array of experiences that will leave you enchanted and hungry to explore more. Don't forget to seek out the hidden treasures, which uncover the city's calmer, more intimate charms, providing a deeper connection to this magnificent location in the heart of the Alps.4.0 Innsbruck

4. CHRISTMAS TRADITIONS

A Tapestry of Festive Delights

Innsbruck, rooted in centuries of history, welcomes the festive season with a rich tapestry of customs that add depth and meaning to the festivities. From dazzling concerts to emotional nativity representations, these traditions infuse the city with a sense of wonder and devotion during the Christmas season.

4.0 Christmas Concerts and Performances

Throughout December, Innsbruck pulses with the lovely notes of Christmas music. The city's cathedrals, symphony halls, and historic venues become stages for stunning performances that capture the true spirit of the season.

1. The Innsbruck Symphony Orchestra: Renowned for its world-class musicianship, the Innsbruck Symphony Orchestra delivers exceptional Christmas concerts that transport audiences through an array of classical and joyful compositions. From famous songs to timeless symphonies, their performances convey a sense of wonder and amazement.

2. Tyrolean Folk Ensembles: Embracing the region's rich musical legacy, Tyrolean folk ensembles take center stage during the festive season. With ancient instruments like the zither and accordion, they build a tapestry of songs that harken back to Tyrol's heritage, producing a sense of warmth and nostalgia.

3. Carol Performances at the Cathedrals: The grand cathedrals of Innsbruck, such as the Cathedral of St. James, serve as beautiful venues for awe-inspiring choral performances. Here,

angelic voices come together to bring to life ageless songs and sacred hymns, infusing the sacred spaces with a transcendent ambiance.

4. Christmas Operettas and Ballets: The city's theaters come alive with charming operettas and ballets that portray uplifting stories of love and redemption, wonderfully capturing the spirit of the season. These performances, sometimes performed against magnificent backdrops, give a genuinely immersive Christmas experience.

4.1 Visiting Local Nativity Scenes

Innsbruck's nativity scenes, or "Krippen" as they are known locally, retain a special place in the hearts of the city's citizens. These exquisite displays represent the Holy Family, shepherds, and the Three Wise Men, all against painstakingly sculpted backdrops that transport visitors to the old Bethlehem.

1. The Tyrolean Folk Art Museum: Home to one of the most extensive and outstanding collections of nativity scenes in the world, the Tyrolean Folk Art Museum is a must-visit for those looking to immerse themselves in this cherished tradition. The amazing craftsmanship and attention to detail in each scene are awe-inspiring.

2. St. Jakob's Basilica: This medieval church offers a renowned nativity scene exhibition that draws visitors from near and far. The sceneries on display range from classic renderings to inventive and artistic adaptations, illustrating the varied ways in which this age-old custom is carried alive.

3. Private Displays in Homes and Galleries: Many Innsbruck residents take great pride in building their nativity scenes, some of which are presented in homes and galleries. These modest exhibits offer a rare peek into the personal interpretations and artistic expressions of this valued ritual.

4. The Altarpiece at the Wilten Basilica*: The Wilten Basilica, with its spectacular baroque interior, is home to an amazing altarpiece representing Nativity. This masterwork of religious art is a tribute to the enduring significance of this sacred story in the hearts of the faithful.

Innsbruck's Christmas traditions, from soul-stirring performances to the magnificence of nativity displays, serve as a monument to the continuing force of the holiday season. These rituals not only enrich the cultural environment of the city but also offer tourists a better appreciation for the genuine spirit of Christmas.

5. CHRISTMAS MARKETS

A Wonderland of Festive Treasures

Innsbruck's Christmas markets are the beating heart of the city's holiday spirit, where centuries-old traditions and the romance of the season come together. These markets are a sensory feast, allowing visitors to browse stalls ornamented with handmade products, sample exquisite seasonal delights, and immerse themselves in the joyous spirit that permeates the city.

5.1 Market Locations and Hours

1. Altstadt Christmas Market
- Location: Located in the heart of the Old Town, in front of the Golden Roof, the Altstadt Christmas Market is a quintessential Innsbruck experience. Its historic setting, with the snow-covered Nordkette mountain range in view, adds to the allure.

- Hours: Open every day from 11:00 AM to 9:00 PM, it allows ample time to leisurely examine the stalls.

2. Marktplatz Market
- Location: Situated in the city's largest square, Marktplatz Market emanates a bustling atmosphere. The towering Christmas tree and the surrounding buildings lit up with festive lights create a lovely environment.

- Hours: This market also operates from 11:00 AM to 9:00 PM, allowing travelers to explore it after a day of sightseeing.

3. Wiltener Platzl Market
- Location: Tucked away in the picturesque district of Wilten, this market offers a more intimate experience. The medieval Wilten Basilica gives a beautiful background to the festivities.
- Hours: Open daily from 3:00 PM to 7:00 PM, it's excellent for an evening stroll through the stalls.

4. Panorama Christkindlmarkt

- Location: Set against the background of the magnificent Nordkette mountain range, the Panorama Christkindlmarkt at Hungerburg guarantees a unique market experience. Accessible via the Hungerburgbahn funicular, it offers amazing views of Innsbruck.

- Hours: Operating from 11:00 AM to 6:30 PM, it's a great site to bask in the winter wonderland view.

5.2 Unique Gifts and Souvenirs Shops

The Christmas markets in Innsbruck are a treasure trove of unique items and mementos. Here, craftsmen and sellers demonstrate their workmanship, offering a selection of interesting things that make for ideal souvenirs or presents.

1. Handcrafted Ornaments and Decorations: Artisans in the markets create exquisite hand-painted ornaments and elaborate decorations that reflect the essence of the season. These items, sometimes created from wood, glass, or metal, serve as beloved recollections of your Innsbruck Christmas.

2. Traditional Tyrolean Apparel: Immerse yourself in the local culture by perusing stalls displaying traditional attire like dirndls and lederhosen. These meticulously crafted clothing not only make for a unique gift but also offer an insight into Tyrolean heritage.

3. Delicacies and Local Treats: Indulge in the flavors of the region with treats like freshly baked gingerbread, aromatic mulled wine, and exquisite chocolates. These exquisite delicacies are not only pleasing to the taste buds but also make for fantastic presents.

4. Artisanal Crafts and Jewelry: Discover a broad assortment of handmade items, from delicately designed jewelry to leather goods and pottery. These one-of-a-kind creations reflect the expertise and creativity of local artists.

5. Tyrolean Music and Instruments: Immerse yourself in the musical legacy of the region with real Tyrolean instruments like the zither or traditional Alpine horns.
These rare items are excellent for music fans or as decorative decorations.

Innsbruck's Christmas markets offer a handpicked range of products and souvenirs, ensuring that you take home not only memories but tangible recollections of your lovely stay in this Austrian winter wonderland.

Explore these marketplaces with a feeling of wonder, and you're sure to unearth treasures that will retain a special place in your heart for years to come.

6. CULINARY DELIGHTS

Indulge in Innsbruck's Festive Flavors

Innsbruck's culinary scene over the festive season is a delicious excursion into the heart of Austrian culture. From substantial comfort foods to delightful sweets, the city's offerings are a reflection of its rich cultural background. Here, we explore the gastronomic pleasures that await you during your Christmas break in Innsbruck.

6.1 Traditional Austrian Holiday Cuisine

1. Wiener Schnitzel: A quintessential Austrian delicacy, Wiener Schnitzel is a breaded and fried veal or pork cutlet. Served with a slice of lemon, lingonberry jam, and a side of potato salad, it's a rich and fulfilling dinner that embodies Austrian comfort food.

2. Kartoffelsalat: This tangy potato salad, prepared with a blend of vinegar, mustard, and oil, is a famous side dish in Austria. It commonly accompanies main meals like Wiener Schnitzel, producing a delicious blend of flavors.

3. Rösti: While primarily Swiss, this crispy potato dish has found its way into Austrian cuisine. Served with various toppings like smoked salmon or mushrooms, it's a savory delight that's sure to tickle your taste buds.

4. Strudel: No Austrian Christmas feast is complete without a slice of strudel. Whether packed with apples, cherries, or savory components like cabbage and bacon, this delicacy demonstrates the culinary artistry of the region.

5. Kaiserschmarrn: A sweet and fluffy pancake, Kaiserschmarrn is a delicacy fit for royalty. Served

with a sprinkling of powdered sugar and a side of plum compote, it's a sumptuous delicacy that encapsulates the essence of Austrian sweets.

6.2 Recommended Restaurants and Cafes

1. Goldener Adler: Nestled in the heart of Innsbruck's Old Town, Goldener Adler is a historic inn and restaurant that gives a taste of authentic Tyrolean cuisine. With its quiet ambiance and cuisine emphasizing local dishes, it's a fantastic venue to immerse yourself in the flavors of the region.

2. Sitzwohl: This family-owned restaurant mixes modern culinary techniques with traditional Tyrolean ingredients. The result is a cuisine that gives a contemporary touch on classic foods, delivering a distinctive dining experience in Innsbruck.

3. Die Wilderin: Known for its commitment to using locally sourced and sustainable ingredients, Die Wilderin is a restaurant that celebrates the wealth of the Tyrolean region. The cuisine features fresh pleasures and unique twists of traditional meals.

4. Café Munding: For a taste of Innsbruck's sweet side, Café Munding is a must-visit. Established in 1803, it's a historic cafe that serves a selection of scrumptious pastries, including their famed strudel, in a picturesque setting overlooking the Golden Roof.

6.3 Wine Tasting and Apres-Ski

Innsbruck offers more than simply gastronomic delights; it's also a sanctuary for wine connoisseurs. Take the opportunity to sample regional wines, including delicate whites and strong reds, in local wine bars and cellars. The Tyrolean region is known for its vineyards, and a wine-tasting trip gives a lovely accompaniment to your holiday.

After a day of touring Innsbruck or hitting the slopes, unwind with an Apres-Ski session. Many bars and taverns in the city offer a dynamic Apres-Ski environment, where you can meet with fellow visitors, hear live music, and drink warm beverages like Glühwein (mulled wine) or a famous Austrian Schnapps.

Innsbruck's culinary environment is a tapestry of flavors that honors both history and innovation. From relishing time-honored recipes to experiencing innovative adaptations, your taste buds are in for a treat. Whether you're feasting on hearty Austrian classics or exploring new culinary pleasures, your eating experiences in Innsbruck will be a memorable part of your holiday festivities.

7. INNSBRUCK NIGHTLIFE

A Vibrant Evening Experience

When the sun sets over the Tyrolean Alps, Innsbruck dons a new persona. The city comes alive with a dynamic nightlife scene, offering something for every nocturnal adventurer. From vibrant bars to intriguing live music venues, Innsbruck ensures that your evenings are as enjoyable as your days.

7.1 Bars and Clubs

1. 360° Bar*: Perched on top of the Rathausgalerien shopping mall, 360° Bar offers panoramic views of Innsbruck. With a large drink

selection and a sophisticated setting, it's the perfect spot to start your night.

2. The Galway Bay Irish Pub: For a taste of Irish hospitality in the heart of the Alps, go no farther than The Galway Bay Irish Pub. Known for its vibrant atmosphere and a broad assortment of beers, this pub is a favorite among residents and visitors alike.

3. Machete Burrito Kartell: This cool location is a combination of a Mexican restaurant and a fashionable bar. With a range of cocktails and a bustling clientele, it's a perfect choice for anyone seeking an exciting evening in Innsbruck.

4. Jimmy's Bar: Located in the Grand Hotel Europa, Jimmy's Bar oozes old-world elegance with its exquisite décor and classic cocktails. It's a classy atmosphere for a smart evening of drinks and discussion.

7.2 Evening Entertainment

1. Metropol Cinema: If you're in the mood for a film, Metropol Cinema provides a broad range of movies, from Hollywood blockbusters to independent flicks. The cinema's antique setting lends an extra dimension of beauty to the experience.

2. Casino Innsbruck: For those feeling lucky, Casino Innsbruck is a premier location. Set against the background of the Nordkette mountains, this stylish casino provides a selection of games, from roulette to poker, along with live entertainment.

7.3 Live Bands

1. Treibhaus: This cultural institution and music venue is a hotspot for live music in Innsbruck.
With a varied selection of bands and performers, Treibhaus promises a diverse spectrum of musical experiences, from jazz to rock and everything in between.

2. Weekender Club: Known for its vibrant live music events, Weekender Club hosts local and international musicians, encompassing a wide spectrum of genres.

Whether you're into indie, punk, or techno music, you're bound to find something that strikes a chord.

Innsbruck's nightlife offers a kaleidoscope of experiences, from vibrant clubs to cultural places that exhibit live music.

Whether you're wanting to dance the night away, have a peaceful drink with a view, or immerse yourself in the local music scene, Innsbruck has something to suit every taste. So, as the stars rise over the Alps, let Innsbruck's dynamic nightlife provide the backdrop for an amazing evening during your Christmas vacation.

8. CHRISTMAS EVE AND NEW YEAR'S EVE CELEBRATIONS

Ringing in the Holidays with Joy and Splendor

Innsbruck's Christmas Eve and New Year's Eve events are lively and spectacular experiences that encapsulate the magic and passion of the festive season. Whether you choose a calm evening by candlelight or a lively countdown with fireworks, Innsbruck provides a selection of celebrations to suit every taste.

Christmas Eve Celebration

As nightfall descends over Innsbruck on Christmas Eve, the city takes on a tranquil and magical ambiance. The cobbled walkways of the Old Town are illuminated by the warm glow of lanterns and twinkling lights, creating a magnificent environment that inspires reflection and celebration.

1. Attend Midnight Mass: Start your Christmas Eve with a visit to one of Innsbruck's historic churches, such as the Cathedral of St. James or the Wilten Basilica. Midnight Mass is a cherished tradition, where the soaring voices of choirs fill the air with timeless hymns, and the nativity tableau comes to life in the flickering candlelight.

2. Stroll around the Old Town: After the service, take a stroll through the magnificently decorated streets of the Old Town. Admire the exquisite nativity scenes, and soak in the festive ambiance generated by the lavish decorations and the aroma of seasonal goodies.

3. A classic Christmas Dinner: Many restaurants and inns in Innsbruck offer special Christmas Eve

menus, offering classic Austrian specialties like roasted goose or luscious venison. These magnificent feasts are a great way to experience the flavors of the season.

8.1 Christmas Day Itineraries

1. Morning: Explore the Christmas Markets

- Begin your Christmas Day with a leisurely visit to Innsbruck's stunning Christmas markets.

Stroll around the vendors, sipping on mulled wine and enjoying local goodies. Admire the homemade presents and decorations, and soak in the joyful mood.

2. Afternoon: Discover the Old Town

- Spend the afternoon touring the ancient Old Town. Visit the Tyrolean Folk Art Museum to see stunning nativity scenes, and marvel at the Golden Roof, a symbol of Innsbruck's rich legacy. Enjoy a traditional Austrian meal at one of the neighborhood eateries.

3. Evening: Attend a Christmas Concert
- Wrap up your Christmas Day with a beautiful concert. Innsbruck's cathedrals and concert halls often hold special events, showcasing stunning versions of classical carols and seasonal music.

Allow the music to transport you to a world of holiday magic.

New Year's Eve Celebration

8.2 New Year's Eve Traditions in Innsbruck

1. First-Footing: A valued tradition in Tyrolean culture, 'First-Footing' includes being the first person to enter a home after the stroke of midnight. The 'first-footer' is considered a portent of good luck for the next year. In many households, this tradition is observed with great excitement, with friends and family members taking turns to be the first to enter one other's homes.

2. The Vienna Philharmonic's New Year's event: While not in Innsbruck proper, this world-renowned event is a beloved tradition for many Austrians. Held in Vienna's Musikverein concert hall, it comprises a repertoire of legendary waltzes and polkas by the Strauss family, setting a happy and celebratory tone for the start of the year.

Best Places to Ring in the New Year

1. Maria-Theresien-Straße: It transforms into a vibrant hub of celebration on New Year's Eve. The street is dotted with stalls offering culinary pleasures and local goods, creating a colorful environment. Crowds congregate here to delight in the celebrations and enjoy live entertainment.

2. Bergisel Ski Jump: For an unrivaled view of Innsbruck's fireworks display, head to the Bergisel Ski Jump. Perched far above the city, this position offers a panoramic panorama that provides a spectacular backdrop for the countdown to the new year.

3. Old Town Squares: The squares in Innsbruck's Old Town, such as the Marktplatz and the Domplatz, come alive on New Year's Eve. They are popular gathering locations for locals and visitors alike. Revelers congregate here to celebrate with live music, dancing, and a lively environment.

Fireworks and Countdown Events

1. Fireworks at Bergisel: The highlight of Innsbruck's New Year's Eve celebration is the stunning fireworks display. Set against the backdrop of the spectacular Nordkette mountains, the fireworks dazzle the night sky with a stunning rainbow of colors. The Bergisel Ski Jump provides a fantastic vantage position for this awe-inspiring event.

2. Countdown Events at Pubs and Clubs: Innsbruck's nightlife scene flourishes on New Year's Eve, with pubs and clubs organizing vibrant countdown events. From luxurious hotel galas to frenetic club celebrations, there are options to fit every inclination. Revelers can dance the night away and toast to the arrival of the new year with fellow celebrants.

3. Silvesterpfad: The Silvesterpfad, or New Year's Eve Trail, brings visitors through numerous spots in the city, each offering a unique experience. From live music and entertainment to gastronomic delights and festive décor, this path gives a dynamic way to discover Innsbruck's New Year's Eve celebrations.

Innsbruck's Christmas Eve and New Year's Eve events offer a great blend of tradition, festivity, and introspection. Whether you prefer a calm and introspective evening or an exuberant countdown with fireworks, Innsbruck has something special in store for every visitor during these enchanting nights. Embrace the joy and magnificence of the festive season in this charming Austrian city.

9. DAY TRIPS & EXCURSIONS

Exploring Beyond Innsbruck

While Innsbruck is a treasure mine of cultural and natural attractions, the surrounding region of Tyrol offers even more chances for travel and discovery. Day tours and excursions from Innsbruck bring up a world of stunning landscapes, quaint communities, and historical places, providing a well-rounded experience for travelers wishing to immerse themselves in the beauty and history of the Austrian Alps.

9.1 Nearby Villages and Towns

1. Hall in Tirol: A short drive from Innsbruck, Hall in Tirol is a beautifully preserved medieval village that transports visitors back in time.

The cobbled alleyways, well-preserved architecture, and picturesque squares offer an insight into the region's rich history. Don't miss the opportunity to explore the Mint Tower, which historically produced some of Europe's finest coins.

2. Seefeld: Nestled in a high plateau surrounded by mountains, Seefeld is a sanctuary for outdoor enthusiasts. In winter, it's a popular destination for cross-country skiing and snowshoeing. In the warmer months, the area offers clean hiking routes and breathtaking views. The village itself has a warm, alpine charm.

3. Hallstatt: Although a bit farther from Innsbruck, Hallstatt is a gem worth the journey. Situated on a gorgeous lake and surrounded by stunning mountains, Hallstatt is generally regarded as one of the most picturesque villages in the world. The UNESCO-listed town features

lovely streets, an intriguing salt mine, and captivating vistas from the Hallstatt Skywalk.

4. Rattenberg: Known as the smallest town in Austria, Rattenberg is a hidden gem just a short drive from Innsbruck. The town's tiny lanes are lined with historic stores, particularly those dealing in glassware and crystal. A visit to the Augustiner Museum offers insight into the region's creative past.

5. Wattens and the Swarovski Crystal Worlds*: Located a short drive from Innsbruck, Wattens is home to the famed Swarovski Crystal Worlds. This multimedia art installation is an immersive experience, highlighting the creative possibilities of crystal. It's a fascinating tour for art and design fans.

6. Schwaz: This old mining town boasts a rich legacy reaching back to the Middle Ages. The Schwaz Silver Mine offers guided tours that provide an insight into the region's mining history. The town's medieval architecture and the beautiful St. Mary's Church are well worth investigating.

These adjacent villages and towns offer a broad range of experiences, from stepping back in time in Hall in Tirol to relishing in the natural beauty of Seefeld. Each stop showcases a unique part of Tyrolean culture, history, and natural grandeur. Whether you're drawn to the charm of ancient alleyways or the appeal of alpine views, these day trips and excursions from Innsbruck promise a rich tapestry of discoveries.

10. PRACTICAL INFORMATION

Navigating Your Innsbruck Journey with Ease

When going on a visit to Innsbruck, it's necessary to have essential practical information at your fingertips. From health services to emergency contacts, currency conversion to cultural standards, being well-informed assures a smooth and pleasurable vacation. Here's a detailed guide to practical facts that can enhance your trip to Innsbruck.

10.1 Health and Medical Services

Innsbruck offers high-quality medical facilities and services for travelers:

1. Hospitals and Medical Centers: In case of emergencies or medical problems, University Hospital Innsbruck (Universitätsklinik für Innere Medizin) and the private Clinic Innsbruck are recognised possibilities.

2. Pharmacies: Pharmacies, known as "Apotheke" in German, are commonly available. Look for the green cross symbol. They normally operate throughout standard business hours, with one or two giving 24-hour services on a rotating basis.

10.2 Emergency Contacts and Services

In case of emergencies, dial:

Medical Emergencies: 112
Police: 133
Fire Department: 122

These numbers are universal throughout Australia and will link you to the right services.

10.3 Travel Insurance

Before your journey, verify you have comprehensive travel insurance. This defends you against unexpected events such as medical emergencies, vacation cancellations, and misplaced possessions. Verify if your policy covers the specific activities you plan to conduct in Innsbruck, such as winter sports.

10.4 Currency and Budgeting

The currency of Austria is the Euro (€). ATMs are commonly distributed in Innsbruck, making it easier to withdraw cash. Credit and debit cards are frequently accepted, but it's good to carry some cash, especially for little purchases or in more isolated places.

10.5 Staying Safe During Your Trip

Innsbruck is considered a safe place for vacationers. However, it's necessary to apply common sense safety practices. Keep an eye on your stuff, especially in crowded settings, and avoid poorly lit or quiet areas at night.

10.6 Language and Communication

German is the official language of Austria, including Innsbruck. While many residents speak English, especially in tourist regions, it's appreciated if you attempt to use simple German words. This demonstrates respect for the native culture.

10.7 Local Customs and Etiquette

1. Greeting: A firm handshake is a typical manner to greet someone. Address persons using their titles and last names until encouraged to use their first names.

2. Punctuality: Punctuality is highly prized in Austrian society. Arriving a few minutes early for appointments or meetings is considered polite.

3. Tipping: Tipping is traditional in Australia. In restaurants, leaving a tip of 5-10% is standard. For other services, including taxis and motels, rounding up the bill is welcomed.

10.8 Useful Phrases in German

Hello: Guten Tag
Goodbye: Auf Wiedersehen

Thank you: Danke
Please: Bitte
Excuse me: Entschuldigung
Yes: Ja
No: Nein
Help: Hilfe
I don't understand: Ich verstehe nicht.
Where's the nearest restroom?: Wo ist die nächste Toilette?
Can you speak English?: Sprechen Sie Englisch?

Having a few basic German phrases at your disposal can go a long way in enriching your interactions and experiences in Innsbruck.

With these practical insights, you'll traverse Innsbruck with confidence and ease, ensuring that your trip is not only enjoyable but also hassle-free. Remember, being well-prepared allows you to fully immerse yourself in the beauty and culture of this wonderful Austrian city.

11. CONCLUSION

As your Innsbruck Christmas holiday draws to an end, you'll bring with you memories of charming marketplaces, festive traditions, and breathtaking Alpine vistas. This Austrian treasure has left an unforgettable impact on your heart, presenting a blend of culture, history, and natural beauty that few destinations can rival.

Making the Most of Your Innsbruck Christmas Vacation

Reflecting on your journey, it's evident that Innsbruck is a city that embraces the holiday season with unrivaled zeal. The Christmas markets, aglow with the warmth of glittering lights, tempt you to browse stalls laden with handcrafted treasures and sample seasonal treats. The nativity scenes, a monument to the region's deep-rooted traditions, generate a sense of awe and devotion.

Venturing beyond the city boundaries, adjacent villages like Hall in Tirol and Seefeld allow you to travel back in time, immersing yourself in the history and charm of Tyrolean life. Each cobbled street and centuries-old building whispers stories of a bygone era, affording a look into the rich past of the Austrian Alps.

Share Your Innsbruck Experiences

Your experiences in Innsbruck are not just treasured recollections but also helpful information for fellow travelers. Consider sharing your adventures through social media, travel blogs, or talks with friends and family. Your recommendations and tips can inspire others to start on their visit to this wonderful Alpine city.

Remember to record the moments that resonated most with you - the dazzling markets, the beautiful mountain panoramas, and the deep connections with people. These images will serve as beloved souvenirs, allowing you to relive the beauty of your Innsbruck Christmas trip for years to come.

As you bid farewell to Innsbruck, know that you're leaving behind a piece of your heart in this gorgeous city. The memories you've built, the places you've seen, and the warmth of the Christmas spirit will long be a part of your travel narrative.

Innsbruck's festive charm and winter beauty will continue to draw people from across the world, inviting them to experience the magic of the Austrian Alps over the Christmas season. Until your next visit, may the spirit of Innsbruck accompany you on your future excursions, reminding you of the beauty and joy that travel brings into your life. Safe travels!

Printed in Great Britain
by Amazon